Finding Forgiveness
with Pope Francis

by
Rev Nick Donnelly

*All booklets are published thanks to the
generous support of the members of the
Catholic Truth Society*

CATHOLIC TRUTH SOCIETY
PUBLISHERS TO THE HOLY SEE

Contents

Author dedication

I dedicate this booklet to John and Vera Burden, and the Burden
family, longtime friends of the Donnelly family.

*All rights reserved. First published 2016 by The Incorporated Catholic
Truth Society, 40-46 Harleyford Road London SE11 5AY Tel: 020 7640
0042 Fax: 020 7640 0046. © 2016 The Incorporated Catholic Truth Society.*

ISBN 978 1 78469 123 3

Foreword

Over the past forty-nine years, serving the Church as a priest and bishop, I have realised that we are living through an age of popes who are great teachers. God chooses to use the personal history and personality of each pope to transmit the Gospel in unique ways to meet the needs of their times. I thought Pope St John Paul II was a courageous and energetic teacher, and Pope Emeritus Benedict XVI was a profound and eloquent teacher. But it's true to say that Pope Francis is even more prolific, with the passion of the prophet Amos. Most mornings the Holy Father teaches through his daily meditations in the chapel of the Domus Sanctae Marthae, and this is on top of addresses at his weekly General Audience and praying the Angelus.

Faced with such a wealth of papal teaching, in such a short period of time, I think it is necessary to have clear guides who can draw out the key insights and themes. This is one of the reasons why I have enjoyed reading the series of articles Deacon Nick Donnelly has written for the Jubilee of Mercy as they came out in the *Catholic Voice Ireland* newspaper, now brought together in this Catholic Truth Society booklet. With his thorough knowledge of the teaching of Pope Francis, and his own theological training, Nick has written a clear and informed guide to the Holy Father's thoughts on sin, mercy, forgiveness and the Sacrament of Confession.

Through Pope Francis's teaching on forgiveness we enter more deeply into the reality evoked in the *Benedictus*, the Canticle of Zechariah, "To make known to his people their salvation through forgiveness of all their sins, the loving kindness of the heart of our God who visits us like the dawn from on high" (*Lk* 1:77-78).

Nick and I have been friends for many years now, since my time as the Bishop of Lancaster when we worked together on my Fit for Mission? initiative. I ordained Nick to the Permanent Diaconate in 2005, and he recently reminded me that in my homily during his ordination I advised him to put his theological education at the service of the people. I'm glad to see all these years later that he is still following my advice!

Patrick O'Donoghue
Bishop Emeritus of Lancaster

Early versions of these chapters were published as a series of articles for the Jubilee Year of Mercy by Catholic Voice Ireland *and* National Catholic Register.

Mercy Makes Sense Only if You Haven't Lost the Sense of Sin

During his 2013 interview returning home from World Youth Day Rio, Pope Francis made an observation overlooked by the media. The Holy Father mentioned the importance of a "theology of sin" to understanding the truth about God's mercy. By this he is not talking about a remote or academic understanding, as is sometimes mistakenly imagined when the word "theology" is used, but a need to have a real sense of our sin if we are to have a real relationship with our merciful God.

His recently published book-length interview with Andrea Tornielli *The Name of God is Mercy* gives an insight into Pope Francis's theology of sin, which provides us with valuable insights into divine mercy.

In this book, Pope Francis highlights the difficulty facing pastors and people discussing the reality of sin and God's merciful offer of forgiveness. In particular, he talks about two types of people - those who have lost the sense of sin, and, those who have lost a sense of God's mercy. Both attitudes are harmful because they stop us encountering the healing grace of God's merciful forgiveness.

Loss of the sense of sin

Early in his interview with Tornielli, Pope Francis refers to a fundamental problem that has been identified and considered by many popes since Venerable Pope Pius XII: the crisis of the loss of a sense of sin. Pope Francis says: "Pius XII, more than half a century ago, said that the tragedy of our age was that it had lost its sense of sin, the awareness of sin."[1]

Here Pope Francis is referring to an observation made by Pope Pius XII in a radio address of 1946:

> Perhaps the greatest sin in the world today is that men have begun to lose the sense of sin. Smother that, deaden it - it can hardly be wholly cut out from the heart of man - let it not be awakened by any glimpse of the God-man dying on Golgotha's cross to pay the penalty of sin.[2]

Likewise Pope St John Paul II identified a "progressive weakening of the sense of sin" the cause of which he identified in a convergence of moral and cultural factors including the "deadening of conscience", the secular loss of the sense of God and an all pervasive relativism (*Reconciliatio et Paenitentia*, 18).

Pope Benedict XVI also warned about a loss of a sense of sin due to the "exclusion of God from public conscience" (Subiaco lecture 2005) and the "dictatorship of relativism" that recognises no authority other than "one's own ego and desires" (Conclave homily, 2005).

Pope Francis also shares Pope St John Paul II and Pope Benedict XVI's concern about the influence of relativism on our sense of sin: "Relativism wounds people too: all things seem equal, all things appear the same."[3] Pope Francis has previously said that the devil seeks to deaden our consciences so that we can't tell right from wrong, which is the hallmark of relativism: "The man ends up destroyed by the well-mannered method the devil uses, by the way the devil convinces him to do things, with relativism: 'But it is not…but it is not much…no, relax, be calm…'"[4]

Loss of the sense of sin in the Church

Furthermore, Pope Francis, like Pope St John Paul II and Pope Benedict XVI, also warns about the disastrous influence of this loss of a sense of sin in the Church. He distinguishes between sinners, who retain a deep sense of sin, and the corrupt, who have lost their sense of sin.

The corrupt are those individuals who arrogantly deny or reject their need for repentance and God's forgiveness, and who make their sin a habit and way of life. The corrupt mistake their sin for "true treasure", justifying themselves and their behaviour. They pretend to be Christian, masking their vices with "good manners, always managing to keep up appearances", leading double lives. Pope Francis gives a shocking example of one of the corrupt:

We cannot be arrogant. It reminds me of a story I heard from a person I used to know, a manager in Argentina. This man had a colleague who seemed to be very committed to a Christian life: he recited the Rosary, he read spiritual writings, and so on. One day the colleague confided, en passant, as if it were of no consequence, that he was having a relationship with his maid. He made it clear that he thought it was something entirely normal. He said that "these people", and by that he meant maids, were there "for that, too". My friend was shocked; his colleague was practically telling him that he believed in the existence of superior and inferior human beings, with the latter destined to be taken advantage of and used, like the maid. I was stunned by that example, despite all my friend's objections, the colleague remained firm and didn't budge an inch. And he continued to consider himself a good Christian because he prayed, he read his spiritual writings every day, and he went to Mass on Sundays. This is arrogance.[5]

However, even though such individuals have hardened their hearts, Pope Francis does not consider the corrupt beyond the mercy of God. Though they are ordinarily immune to contrition and remorse, the Holy Father has observed that God attempts to save them through "life's great ordeals", which break their hard hearts, opening them to God's grace.

Loss of the sense of God's mercy

The other group particularly identified by Pope Francis are Christians who do not seek God's mercy even though, unlike the corrupt, they have a painful awareness of their sin and their woundedness. These all share in common the failure to seek God's mercy due to losing touch with the true Christian sense of God's merciful love for sinners.

According to Pope Francis there are those Christians who don't want God's mercy because they suffer from a "narcissistic illness", clinging to their woundedness because it gives them the unhealthy pleasure of bitterness: "Or maybe you prefer your wounds, the wounds of sin, and you behave like a dog, licking your wounds with your tongue. This is a narcissistic illness that makes people bitter. There is pleasure in feeling bitter, an unhealthy pleasure."[6]

Another group of Christians don't seek God's mercy because they make the error of believing that their sins are so evil that God will not forgive them: "Today we add further to the tragedy by considering our illness, our sins, to be incurable, things that cannot be healed or forgiven."[7]

Pope Francis refers to these people as those who have come to the erroneous conclusion that they are too great a sinner to encounter Jesus. He recalls his conversations with them:

"But Father, you know that for me, this journey, it's a brutal journey. I'm a great sinner. I've committed many sins. How can I meet Jesus?"… You know that the people Jesus sought out the most were the biggest sinners… Jesus sees our sins… And in our journey - ours, we're all sinners, all of us - when we make mistakes, when we sin, Jesus comes even then, and he forgives us. And this forgiveness that we receive in Confession is a meeting with Jesus.[8]

One of the key messages of Pope Francis's *The Name of God is Mercy* is that there is no sin, there is no habit of sin, there is no relapse into sin, which is beyond the mercy of God:

There are no situations we cannot get out of; we are not condemned to sink into quicksand, in which the more we move the deeper we sink. Jesus is there, his hand extended, ready to reach out to us and pull us out of the mud, out of sin, out of the abyss of evil into which we have fallen. We need only be conscious of our state, be honest with ourselves, and not lick our wounds. We need to ask for the grace to recognise ourselves as sinners.[9]

A healthy sense of sin and mercy

Another theme that runs throughout *The Name of God is Mercy* is Pope Francis's candid admission that he is a sinner. Since he was asked the question during an interview, "Who is Jorge Mario Bergoglio?", Pope Francis has not been shy about identifying himself as a sinner:

"I do not know what might be the most fitting description...
I am a sinner. This is the most accurate definition. It is not
a figure of speech, a literary genre. I am a sinner."[10]

The Holy Father encourages us - sometimes gently,
sometime forcefully - to seek the grace to make the same
honest and frank admission, because he knows from
personal experience that knowing and admitting that we
are sinners will liberate and transform our lives.

In answer to Andrea Torniella's question, "How do we
recognise that we ourselves are sinners? What would you
say to someone who doesn't feel like one?", Pope Francis
answered:

> I would advise him to ask for the grace of feeling like
> one! Yes, because even recognising oneself as a sinner is
> a grace. It is a grace that is granted to you. Without that
> grace, the most one can say is: I am limited, I have my
> limits, these are my mistakes. But recognising oneself
> as a sinner is something else. It means standing in front
> of God, who is our everything, and presenting him with
> our selves, which are our nothing. Our miseries, our
> sins. What we need to ask for is truly an act of grace.[11]

Sinners are those individuals who have the humility and
sense of woundedness to admit that they are weak and in
need of God's mercy and forgiveness. Pope Francis believes
that one can be a great sinner, but not fall into corruption.
Pointing to the examples of Zacchaeus, Matthew, the

Samaritan woman at the well and Nicodemus, the Holy
Father says their sinful hearts were open to God's mercy:

> Their sinful hearts all had something that saved them
> from corruption. They were open to forgiveness, their
> hearts felt their own weakness, and that small opening
> allowed the strength of God to enter. When a sinner
> recognises himself as such, he admits in some way that
> what he was attached to, clings to, is false.[12]

What is sin?

In order to place us in a position to admit our attachment to
what is false, Pope Francis undertakes a basic catechesis
on the nature of sin. This is urgently needed in Western
culture, so heavily influenced by Sigmund Freud and
Carl Jung as to be in a state of denial about the objective
reality of sin and dangerously attracted to embracing the
demonic shadow.

It shouldn't surprise us that as a consequence of his
formation as a Jesuit, Pope Francis has no problem talking
in stark and explicit terms about the evil represented
by our sins. The First Week of St Ignatius of Loyola's
Spiritual Exercises commences with a meditation on the
catastrophic damage caused by angelic and human sin.
Pope Francis likewise wants us to truly look at the dark
reality of sin in the light of God's mercy, because without
God's mercy such knowledge would be overwhelmingly
harmful. He wants us to take responsibility for our sin.

When asked why we are sinners Pope Francis answers very simply, "Because of original sin"; our nature "is wounded by original sin":

> It's something we know from experience. Our humanity is wounded; we know how to distinguish between good and evil, we know what is evil, we try to follow the path of goodness, but we often fall because of our weaknesses and choose evil. This is a consequence of original sin…something that actually happened at the origins of mankind".[13]

The Holy Father doesn't pull his punches about the evil nature of our sin compared to the goodness of God. Our sins not only wound us, and damage our relationships, our sins also "displease God" and we should be displeased with what displeases God. Quoting the Church Fathers, Pope Francis writes that knowing that our sins displease God should shatter our hearts: "The Church Fathers teach us that a shattered heart is most pleasing to God. It is the sign that we are conscious of our sins, of the evil we have done, of our wretchedness, and of our need for forgiveness and mercy."[14]

This is why Pope Francis views our sin from the perspective of the ancient Tradition of the Easter Exultet with its shocking praise of Adam and Eve's catastrophic sin as a *'felix culpa'* [a happy fault]. The Holy Father knows that an honest knowledge of our sin and our need for God's mercy will lead us to experience the love of "so great, so glorious a Redeemer".

Some questions to ask ourselves

- Have I done my best to have a healthy sense of sin and mercy, neither losing a sense of sin, nor considering myself so sinful that I cannot be saved?

- Have I asked for the grace to be able to feel my sin, and, as a sinner, stand in front of God and ask him for my needs - for mercy, for forgiveness?

- Have I reflected on the dark reality of sin in the light of God's mercy?

Change the Way You See and
Live Forgiveness

During his first Angelus as pope in St Peter's Square, and in *The Name of God is Mercy*, Pope Francis tells the story of his encounter with an old woman just after his appointment as an auxiliary bishop of Buenos Aires. This story helps explain why mercy and forgiveness are the primary focus of his pontificate:

> An elderly woman approached me, humble, very humble, and over eighty years old. I looked at her, and I said, "Grandmother," - because in our country that is how we address the elderly - "do you want to make your confession?" "Yes", she said to me. "But if you have not sinned…" And she said to me: "We all have sins…" "But perhaps the Lord does not forgive them." "The Lord forgives all things", she said to me with conviction. "But how do you know, Madam?" "If the Lord did not forgive everything, the world would not exist." I felt an urge to ask her: "Tell me, Madam, did you study at the Gregorian [University]?", because that is the wisdom which the Holy Spirit gives: inner wisdom focused on God's mercy.[15]

Pope Francis explains why the grandmother's words made such an impression on him: "I was struck by the woman's words: without mercy, without God's forgiveness, the world would not exist; it couldn't exist." Since this encounter, when Pope Francis looks at the world, he sees the vastness of the earth, the multitudes of peoples, himself and each individual upheld in 'being' by God's forgiveness. We live and move and have our being in God's forgiveness.

We are made for forgiveness

By giving primacy to forgiveness in God's relationship with creation, Pope Francis is returning to an ancient insight of the Church Fathers. To this end, the Holy Father, the day after inaugurating the Jubilee of Mercy, expressed the hope that we would change the way we see and live forgiveness. He further developed his insight into the existence of the world depending on God's forgiveness by quoting from St Ambrose:

St Ambrose, in a theological book that he wrote about Adam, takes up the story of the creation of the world and says that each day after God made something - the moon, the sun or the animals - [the Bible] says: "God saw that it was good". But when he made man and woman, the Bible says: "He saw that it was very good". St Ambrose asks himself: "Why does he say 'very good'? Why is God so content after the creation of man and woman?" Because finally he had someone to forgive. (Cf. St Ambrose, *The Hexameron*).[16]

This does not mean that God planned or intended man to be a sinner, or wants him to remain a sinner. On the contrary: being omniscient, God knew before creation the whole history of man's sin. But more than just seeing man's sin, he viewed this history of sin through the love he has for his Beloved Son, true God and true man. Knowing that man would sin, and that his Son would die on the cross to redeem man, God created the universe within the reality of his act of forgiveness in which he sent his Son.

During the Year of Mercy Pope Francis wants us to see the world and ourselves with new eyes, with minds and hearts alive to the intrinsic primacy of forgiveness. After this Jubilee Pope Francis hopes that Christians will never again make forgiveness the overlooked virtue of Christian life, neglected and ignored in the way we live our lives.

This Jubilee, in other words, is a privileged moment for the Church to learn to choose only "what pleases God most". What is it that "pleases God most"? Forgiving his children, having mercy on them, so that they may in turn forgive their brothers and sisters, shining as a flame of God's mercy in the world. This is what pleases God most.[17]

If we adopt Pope Francis's teaching on the intrinsic primacy of forgiveness in creation it will transform our understanding and experience of praying the Lord's Prayer. "Forgive us our trespasses as we forgive those who trespass against us" becomes essential to how we define ourselves. We will see ourselves as made for forgiveness, as orientated to forgiveness at the level of being. We will come to see being unforgiving and merciless as a repudiation of our own nature and the purpose of the universe.

If you don't forgive you're not Christian

Pope Francis's understanding of the primacy of forgiveness explains why he cautions that if we aren't forgiving then we are not Christian:

> If you can't forgive, you are not a Christian. You may be a good man, a good woman but you are not doing what Our Lord did. What's more, if you can't forgive, you cannot receive the peace of the Lord. And every day when we pray the 'Our Father': Forgive us as we have forgiven those… It's a condition.[18]

It's not enough to seek forgiveness for our sins from God through the Sacrament of Confession to be an authentic Christian, we also need to genuinely forgive those who injure and hurt us:

> Jesus teaches us to pray to the Father in this way: "Forgive us our debts as we forgive our debtors." If I

am not able to forgive, then I am not able to ask for forgiveness. "But, Father, I confess, I go to Confession." "And what do you do before you confess?" "Well, I think of the things I did wrong." "Alright." "Then I ask the Lord for forgiveness and promise not to do those things again." "Okay…and then go to the priest? Before you do, however, you're missing something: have you forgiven those who have hurt you?"[19]

Pope Francis goes so far as to warn that if we don't forgive others with all our heart then we can't really benefit from the forgiveness of God because our lack of forgiveness means we don't really open our hearts to his forgiveness: "God always forgives, always - but he asks me to forgive [others]. If I do not forgive, in a sense, I close the door to God's forgiveness. 'Forgive us our debts as we forgive our debtors.'"[20]

Why is it so hard to forgive?

Pope Francis would be the last person to encourage the type of 'polite' forgiveness that we occasionally come across in the Church. When offended or angered there is pressure to say "forget about it" or "there's nothing to forgive" because it's expected of Christians. However, such polite forgiveness can often prove itself insincere, with the conflict, and accompanying resentment, remaining unresolved, damaging relationships. Such dishonest 'forgiveness' given out of a sense of politeness can block us from genuine forgiveness.

Also, Pope Francis is not naive about our capacity to express genuine forgiveness, damaged as it is by original sin and concupiscence. Our innate capacity for forgiveness is so often blocked by our refusal to let go of "anger, wrath, violence, and revenge" (*Misericordiae Vultus,* 9). In a culture that puts a premium on assertiveness, competition and 'not losing face' there is an inhibition against publicly admitting our need to forgive and be forgiven. Pope Francis's frequent public requests for forgiveness from Protestant communities and non-Christians is an attempt to break through this taboo.

The Holy Father once posted on Twitter: "It is hard to forgive others. Lord, grant us your mercy, so that we can always forgive." This papal tweet expresses a simple truth - that we can only genuinely forgive others if we have ourselves experienced God's mercy and forgiveness.

How do we forgive others?

Over the past three years Pope Francis has provided a catechesis on how to forgive others that will help us realise his hopes for the Jubilee of Mercy. Before anything else we must ask "for the grace to understand that without mercy a person cannot do a thing, cannot do a single thing, that 'the world would not exist'".[21]

Pope Francis also thinks it's important that we distinguish between phoney forgiveness and real forgiveness. Forgiveness must not be confused with excusing or overlooking the sinfulness of ourselves and others. Reflecting on the prophet Azariah beseeching the Lord's forgiveness on Israel (*Dn* 3:25, 34-43) Pope Francis pointed out:

> Azariah does not say to the Lord: "Sorry, we made a mistake". In fact, asking forgiveness is something else, it's not the same as making an apology. These are two different things: the first is simply asking to be excused, the second involves the acknowledgement of having sinned. Indeed, sin is not simply a mistake. Sin is idolatry, it is worshipping the many idols that we have: pride, vanity, money, the self, wellbeing. This is why Azariah doesn't simply apologise but begs forgiveness.[22] Forgiveness must be asked sincerely, whole-heartedly - and forgiveness must be given whole-heartedly to those, who have injured us.[23]

Forgiving our family and friends

The daily practice of apologising for the hurt and upset we cause to others is vital in creating a culture of forgiveness in our homes, parishes and workplaces:

> We wrong one another every day. We must take into account these mistakes, due to our frailty and our selfishness. However, what we are asked to do is to promptly heal the wounds that we cause, to immediately reweave the bonds that break within the family. If we

wait too long, everything becomes more difficult. There is a simple secret to healing wounds and to avoiding recriminations. It's this: do not let the day end without apologising, without making peace between husband and wife, between parents and children, brothers and sisters…between daughters- and mothers-in-law! If we learn to apologise promptly and to give each other mutual forgiveness, the wounds heal, the marriage grows stronger and the family becomes an increasingly stronger home, which withstands the shocks of our smaller or greater misdeeds. This is why there is no need for a long speech, as a caress is enough: one caress and everything is over and one can start afresh. But do not end the day at war![24]

How many families have been torn apart, parents and children estranged from each other, because of the failure to forgive? How many parishes divided into warring cliques because slights and bruised egos become entrenched dislike and hostility due to a lack of forgiveness?

Forgiving our enemies

And there is the practice of forgiveness that goes beyond forgiving members of our family whom we love - forgiving our enemies - the people who intentionally mean us harm in some form or other. How do we forgive our enemies, those who hate us? Pope Francis holds up St Stephen, the martyr and deacon, as the exemplar of forgiving enemies.

St Stephen shows us that the true disciple of Christ lives his words of forgiveness from the cross: "Father, forgive them, for they do not know what they are doing" (*Lk* 23:34). Likewise, Stephen "knelt down and cried with a loud voice: 'Lord, do not hold this sin against them'" (*Ac* 7:60). Pope Francis concludes:

> Forgiving, however, is not an easy thing, it is always very difficult. How can we imitate Jesus? From what point do we begin to pardon the small and great wrongs that we suffer each day? First of all, beginning with prayer, as St Stephen did. We begin with our own heart: with prayer we are able to face the resentment we feel, by entrusting to God's mercy those who have wronged us: "Lord, I ask you for him, I ask you for her". Then we discover that this inner struggle to forgive cleanses us of evil, and that prayer and love free us from the interior chains of bitterness. It is so awful to live in bitterness! Every day we have the opportunity to practise forgiving, to live a gesture so lofty that it brings man closer to God. Like our heavenly Father, may we too become merciful, because through forgiveness, we conquer evil with good, we transform hatred into love and in this way we make the world cleaner.[25]

There is no better time than now to ask Our Lord for the grace to forgive others, especially those who have deeply hurt us, entrusting them to God's mercy. We are made for forgiveness.

Some questions to ask ourselves

- Have I done my best to forgive others and so truly pray "forgive us our trespasses as we forgive others who trespass against us"?

- Is my forgiveness 'genuine' - letting go of anger, violence and revenge?

- Do I do my best to make sure I do not let the day end without asking forgiveness and making peace?

- Do I follow Pope Francis's steps for genuine forgiveness:

  - realise that the world would not exist without God's mercy;
  - ask for the grace to feel my sin;
  - sincerely, whole-heartedly recognise that I have sinned and beg God's mercy and forgiveness;
  - ask for grace to let go of my feelings of anger, violence or revenge against others;
  - entrust to God's mercy those who have wronged me: "Lord, I ask you for him, I ask you for her";
  - sincerely, whole-heartedly grant forgiveness to others?

Why Does Pope Francis Say the Name of God Is Mercy?

When you reflect on it, Pope Francis's first book published as pope, *The Name of God is Mercy*, has a title that can startle and challenge like one of Our Lord's parables. A parable is meant to shake up the listener to see reality from God's perspective, overturning safe assumptions and breaking through unthinking conventions. "The Name of God is Mercy" is a challenging title because if there's one thing most Catholics assume they know, it's the names of God - YHWH, the Lord, Our Lord Jesus Christ, Saviour, the Most Holy Trinity, God the Father, God the Son and God the Holy Spirit.

Pope Francis doesn't want us to make the grave mistake of thinking that we know who God is, just because we know his name. It's dangerous to think we can label God and store him away safely just because we know his name. The Holy Father has warned us on a number of occasions to have the "apostolic courage to live life and not to make a museum of memories of our Christian life". To acknowledge that the name of God is mercy is not meant to replace or supplant the names of God given to us by Sacred Scripture and sacred Tradition, but to help us enter more deeply into the life-giving, life-transforming mystery of God.

Pope Francis is not the first with the insight into God's name as 'mercy', though he is the first to give it such prominence. He acknowledges the debt he owes to Pope Emeritus Benedict XVI for this insight.[26] On 30th March 2008 Pope Benedict XVI said during a Regina Cæli address:

> Indeed, mercy is the central nucleus of the Gospel message; it is the very name of God, the Face with which he revealed himself in the Old Covenant and fully in Jesus Christ, the Incarnation of creative and redemptive Love. May this merciful love also shine on the face of the Church and show itself through the Sacraments.

God reveals his name

It is important to stress that God reveals his name to man, man does not name God. There are many events in Salvation History where God reveals his name - the theophanies on Mount Sinai to Moses; the Annunciation to the Blessed Virgin Mary at Nazareth; the theophanies at Our Lord's Baptism and Transfiguration: "This is my Beloved Son"; and Our Lord's promise to send the Holy Spirit (*Jn* 14:26).

These revelations of the Divine Name are, in themselves, acts of divine mercy, because we are saved by God's Holy Name: "And there is salvation in no one else, for there is no other name under heaven given among men by which we must be saved" (*Ac* 4:12). In biblical culture to disclose one's personal name was an act of intimacy establishing a life-changing communion. To know God means to encounter a personal reality, and a person is not known unless his name is known (Fr John McKenzie SJ, *Dictionary of the Bible*). God's decision to bestow a name on himself is a profoundly merciful act that prepares for the Incarnation because by giving his name he makes himself available for personal relationships with sinful men and women.

God reveals his name as mercy

Pope Francis locates God's revelation of his name as mercy during one of the theophanies to Moses on Mount Sinai, where God first revealed his mysterious name: "I AM WHO AM" (*Ex* 3:13-14). Following the liberation of the Hebrew tribes from slavery in Egypt, Moses led them to Mount Sinai where God again revealed himself following Israel's blasphemous and idolatrous worship of the Golden Calf:

> And the Lord descended in the cloud and stood with him there, and proclaimed the name of the Lord. The Lord passed before him, and proclaimed, "The Lord, the Lord, a God merciful and gracious, slow to anger, and abounding in steadfast love and faithfulness, keeping steadfast love for thousands, forgiving iniquity and transgression and sin (*Ex* 34:5-7).

The disclosure of God's name prior to, and during, the events of the Exodus, associates forevermore the name of the Lord with his merciful acts of salvation and liberation. The *Catechism of the Catholic Church* describes this link of the revelation of God's name as "I AM" with the revelation of his loving forgiveness as expressing God's constant and faithful mercy towards sinful man (*CCC* 211). This connection between God's faithfulness and mercy is very important to Pope Francis and his theology of God's name:

> In Sacred Scripture, the Lord is presented as a "merciful God." This is his name with which he reveals to us, so to say, his face and his heart. He himself, as the book of Exodus recounts, reveals himself to Moses, calling himself "The Lord, a God merciful and gracious, slow to anger and abounding in steadfast love and faithfulness" (*Ex* 34:6)… Faithfulness in mercy is the very being of God. And that is why this God is totally and forever reliable. A strong and stable presence. This is the certainty of our faith.[27]

The maternal mercy of God

The mercy of God expressed by the disclosure of his name is so intimate and so tender that Scripture uses maternal imagery to convey its reality in our lives. God's loving kindness is described in terms of vulnerable, heartfelt affection: "My heart recoils within me; my compassion grows warm and tender" (*Ho* 11:8). Jesus expresses his mercy towards his enemies in Jerusalem with the tenderness of a mother: "O Jerusalem, Jerusalem, killing the prophets and stoning those who are sent to you! How often would I have gathered your children together as a hen gathers her brood under her wings, and you would not!" (*Lk* 13:34)

Aware of the importance of these maternal images in Scripture, Pope Francis uses them to convey the tender reality of mercy associated with God's name:

> The Lord is "merciful": this word evokes a tender approach like that of a mother towards her child. Indeed, the Hebrew term used in the Bible evokes the viscera or even the maternal womb. Therefore, the image it suggests is that of a God who is moved and who softens for us like a mother when she takes her child in her arms, wanting only to love, protect, help, ready to give everything, even herself. This is the image that this term evokes. A love, therefore, which can be defined in the best sense as 'visceral'.[28]

God's offer of intimate communion through the merciful disclosure of his name to sinful man is not a static event relegated to the past, but is the offer of a dynamic, transformative relationship that challenges sinful man to think and behave like God. Receiving God's tender, heartfelt forgiveness we are meant to show the same maternal forgiveness to others in our lives.

The Church as a merciful mother

This is one of the reasons why Pope Francis often emphasises the Church's role as a tender mother in our lives, particularly as the sign and agent of God's mercy. This appreciation of the maternal nature of the Church goes back to early Christianity. For example, the font was seen as the womb of the Church that gave new life to the baptised. Another reason why Pope Francis appreciates the maternal nature of the Church is his relationship with his own mother, Regina Maria. He recounts how his mother, whom he describes as having the gift of counsel, advised him to go to Our Lady whenever he had problems: "She did not know how to solve her son's problems, but she indicated the right way: 'Go to Our Lady and she'll tell you.'"

Pope Francis explains that now is the time for the Church to show her maternal love for sinners:

> Yes, I believe that this is a time of mercy. The Church is showing her maternal side, her motherly face, to a humanity that is wounded. She does not wait for the wounded to knock on her doors, she looks for them on the streets, she gathers them in, she embraces them, she takes care of them, she makes them feel loved.[29]

Jesus is the face of the Father's mercy

When Pope Francis writes that "Jesus Christ is the face of the Father's mercy" he is taking us deeper into the mystery of God. The truth of the Incarnation is that the words and deeds of Jesus reveal the mystery of God:

> Christ's whole earthly life - his words and deeds, his silences and sufferings, indeed his manner of being and speaking - is *Revelation* of the Father. Jesus can say: "Whoever has seen me has seen the Father", and the Father can say: "This is my Son, my Chosen; listen to him!" Because Our Lord became man in order to do his Father's will, even the least characteristics of his mysteries manifest "God's love … among us" (*CCC* 516).

Christ is the definitive expression of the mystery of God, revealing the invisible God in the flesh. He manifests the saving plan of God because he is, in his own person, the presence of God and his deeds are the fulfilment of that plan. His words and deeds are integral mysteries.

Christ's mysteries are not dead history, but living realities that we can share in now through faith and the Sacraments. Our participation in his mysteries was the whole purpose of the Incarnation, so that we would come to share the divine nature. Pope Francis wants us to enter more deeply into the mysteries of the Father's mercy incarnated by Christ.

Jesus reveals his abyss of mercy

Pope Francis uses an unusual phrase to describe the profound mystery of mercy revealed in Jesus: the "abyss of mercy".

It is not easy to entrust oneself to God's mercy, because it is an abyss beyond our comprehension. But we must! … "Oh, I am a great sinner!" "All the better! Go to Jesus: he likes you to tell him these things!" He forgets, he has a very special capacity for forgetting. He forgets, he kisses you, he embraces you and he simply says to you: "Neither do I condemn you; go, and sin no more" (*Jn* 8:11).

Pope Francis's use of "the abyss of mercy" to describe divine mercy can be traced back to the Saint of Mercy, Faustina Kowalska. Pope Francis signalled the influence of St Faustina on his understanding of mercy, choosing the vigil of the Feast of Divine Mercy to issue his papal bull decreeing the Jubilee of Mercy. St Faustina relates the following locutions from Our Lord in her diary: "This immense love and abyss of mercy are made known in the Incarnation of the Word and in the Redemption" (*Diary* 180); "Let the greatest sinners place their trust in my mercy. They have the right before others to trust in the abyss of my mercy" (*Diary* 1146).

The word "abyss" is used here in the sense that God's mercy is limitless, unfathomable and without end. An abyss is also an image of hidden depths and profound, overwhelming mystery.

Pope Francis also uses another of St Faustina's phrases to convey the limitless, unfathomable nature of divine mercy: "ocean of mercy". The Holy Father contrasts the human torrent of sin and abyss of misery with the immensity of God's abyss and ocean of mercy: "A torrent of misery, swollen by sin, seems to contradict the fullness of time brought by Christ… And yet this swollen torrent is powerless before the ocean of mercy which floods our world. All of us are called to immerse ourselves in this ocean."[30]

Jesus's wounds of mercy

Pope Francis seeks to draw our attention to one of the most personal and intimate mysteries of Christ through which we encounter the mercy of God - the precious wounds of Our Lord. Nothing better conveys the healing mercy of God than the wounds suffered by Our Lord during his Passion and death: "He himself bore our sins in his body on the tree, that we might die to sin and live to righteousness. By his wounds you have been healed. For you were straying like sheep, but have now returned to the Shepherd and Guardian of your souls" (*1 P* 2:24-25).

Since the time of St Bernard and St Francis of Assisi, Catholics have found forgiveness and mercy through devotion to the Five Sacred Wounds of Our Lord. Pope Francis wants us to share that devotion:

The Lord shows us, through the Gospel, his wounds. They are wounds of mercy. It is true: the wounds of Jesus are wounds of mercy… Jesus invites us to behold these wounds, to touch them as Thomas did, to heal our

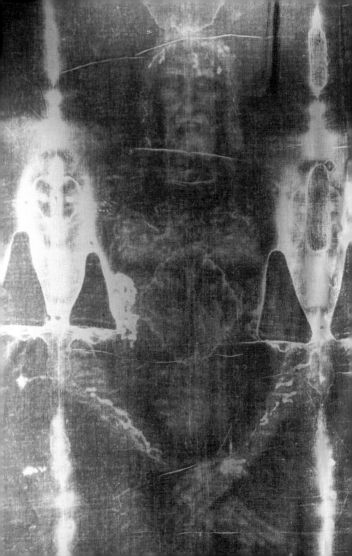

lack of belief. Above all, he invites us to enter into the mystery of these wounds, which is the mystery of his merciful love.[31]

Pope Francis and the Holy Shroud of Turin

Pope Francis has a devotion to Christianity's most precious relic of Our Lord's wounds - the Holy Shroud of Turin. One of his first acts as pope was to record a meditation to introduce an Italian TV broadcast on the Shroud on Easter Saturday. The Holy Father clearly sees the Holy Shroud as an icon of God's mercy:

By means of the Holy Shroud, the unique and supreme Word of God comes to us: Love made man, incarnate in our history; the merciful Love of God who has taken upon himself all the evil of the world to free us from its power. This disfigured face resembles all those faces of men and women marred by a life which does not respect their dignity, by war and violence which afflict the weakest... And yet, at the same time, the face in the Shroud conveys a great peace; this tortured body expresses a sovereign majesty. It is as if it let a restrained but powerful energy within it shine through, as if to say: have faith, do not lose hope; the power of the love of God, the power of the Risen One overcomes all things.[32]

And during the display of the Shroud in 2015 Pope Francis said to pilgrims in St Peter's Square: "I hope that this act of veneration may help us all to find in Jesus Christ the Merciful Face of God, and to recognise it also in the faces of our brothers and sisters, especially those suffering most."[33]

By teaching us that the name of God is mercy Pope Francis invites us to enter into mercy as a profound mystery of God that has many dimensions - maternal, unfathomable, limitless, personal, intimate and healing. Now is the time to show this mercy to wounded humanity.

Some questions to ask ourselves

- God calls me to be part of his holy Church. Have I done my best to show the maternal, motherly face of the Church to those who are wounded? Have I made them feel loved?

- Do I do my best to share and enter into Christ's mysteries - the mysteries of the Father's mercy incarnated by Christ?

- Do I have devotion to the Five Sacred Wounds of Our Lord?

My crucified Jesus,
I kiss the wounds in your Sacred Head
With sorrow deep and true
May every thought in my mind today
Be an act of love for you.

My crucified Jesus,
I kiss the wounds in your Sacred Hands
With sorrow deep and true
May every touch of my hands today
Be an act of love for you.

My crucified Jesus,
I kiss the wounds in your Sacred Feet
With sorrow deep and true
May every step I take today
Be an act of love for you.

My crucified Jesus,
I kiss the wounds in your Sacred Shoulder
With sorrow deep and true
May every cross I bear today
Be an act of love for you.

My crucified Jesus,
I kiss the wounds in your Sacred Heart
With sorrow deep and true
May every beat of my heart today
Be an act of love for you.

Let God's Forgiveness Heal Your Heart

Pope Francis asks us to put aside the illusions of power and strength that are so popular in our society and admit our personal woundedness, the wounds in our families and the wounds in society. He knows that it is only by acknowledging our wounds that we can let God's forgiveness heal our hearts. If we are unable or incapable of admitting our woundedness then we cut ourselves off from God's merciful offer of salvation and redemption.

In *The Name of God is Mercy* Pope Francis makes it clear that he wants to break through the delusion of the super man, who thinks he has no need for God and his healing love. When asked by his interviewer why humanity is in such great need of mercy, Pope Francis answered:

> Because humanity is wounded, deeply wounded. Either it does not know how to cure its wounds or it believes that it's not possible to cure them. And it's not just a question of social ills or people wounded by poverty, social exclusion, or one of the many slaveries of the third millennium. Relativism wounds people too: all things seem equal, all things appear the same. Humanity needs mercy and compassion. Pius XII, more than half a century ago, said that the tragedy of our age was that

it had lost its sense of sin, the awareness of sin. Today we add further to the tragedy by considering our illness, our sins, to be incurable, things that cannot be healed or forgiven.[34]

Humanity is wounded

As a pastor with personal experience of the suffering of so many different people Pope Francis knows that humanity is deeply wounded. His favourite image of the Church as a "field hospital" derives from his familiarity with the wounded nature of man:

> I see the Church as a field hospital after battle. It is useless to ask a seriously injured person if he has high cholesterol and about the level of his blood sugars. You have to heal his wounds. Then we can talk about everything else. Heal the wounds, heal the wounds… And you have to start from the ground up.[35]

During the Vigil of Prayer on the eve of the 2014 Extraordinary Synod on the Family, Pope Francis prayed that the Synod would seek to "heal bleeding wounds, and rekindle hope".

These wounds are the sins that we commit, our sinful habits, our unconfessed sins, and Pope Francis rightfully sees them as deadly threats to ourselves, our families and society. He calls them our "inner wounds, our sins" that remain life-threatening as long as they remain hidden due to being unrepented, unconfessed and unforgiven.

In an address to the Focolare Movement the Holy Father listed the variety of wounds afflicting people:

> It hurts the heart when, before a church, before a humanity with so many wounds, moral wounds, existential wounds, wounds of war, which we all hear of every day, to see that Christians begin to do philosophical, theological, spiritual "byzantinism", rather what is needed is a spirituality of going-out. Go out with this spirituality: do not remain securely locked inside. This is not good. This is "byzantinism"! Today we have no right to byzantinistic reflection. We must go out! Because - I have said this many times - the Church seems like a field hospital. And when one goes to a field hospital, the first task is to heal the wounded, not to measure cholesterol... this will come later... Is this clear?[36]

The original wound

Pope Francis is clear that each one of us is wounded by original sin, a personal sin committed at the beginning of human history by our first parents. This original sin has resulted in the human race's fall from grace and our being changed for the worse in body and soul. The Book of Genesis points back to the origin of this wound that we encounter in ourselves and over which we have no control, except through the sacramental grace of Baptism and the Sacraments. This is how Pope Francis describes our original wound:

Why are we sinners? Because of original sin. It's something we know from experience. Our humanity is wounded; we know how to distinguish between good and evil, we know what is evil, we try to follow the path of goodness, but we often fall because of our weaknesses and choose evil. This is a consequence of original sin, which we are fully aware of thanks to the Book of Revelation. The story of Adam and Eve, the rebellion against God described in the Book of Genesis, uses a richly imaginative language to explain something that actually happened at the origins of mankind.[37]

Looking around we know the world and ourselves aren't how they should be, that our lives are damaged by a history of sin, which God reveals in the Book of Genesis, that goes back to the very beginning of the human race. The first human beings, tempted by the devil, let their trust in the Creator die in their hearts and, abusing their freedom, disobeyed God's command (*Gn* 3:1-11; *Rm* 5:19). After the first sin, the world is virtually inundated by sin (*CCC* 397-401).

The history of the human race since the first sin has been a history of living and dying from the consequences of this wound. The tragedy is that we know deep in our hearts that things could have been so different.

The sanctifying grace of Baptism forgives and frees us from original sin, and frees us from the punishment due to original sin. However, the after-effects of original sin remain, which the Church calls *concupiscence*, or metaphorically, "the tinder for sin". Mgr Ronald Knox described this innate tendency to commit sin, and this innate attraction to evil, using the image of the corner of a book turned down to mark a page. He observed that no matter how many times he straightened the page out, in time the corner would turn down again. Once damaged, always damaged.

The permanent damage caused by original sin is the reason why Pope Francis encourages us to call on Our Lady to help us resist our wounded nature - because she is free from original sin:

> In the Immaculate Conception of Mary we are invited to recognise the dawn of the new world, transformed by the salvific work of the Father and of the Son and of the Holy Spirit. The dawn of the new creation brought about by divine mercy. For this reason the Virgin Mary, never infected by sin and always full of God, is the mother of a new humanity. She is the mother of the recreated world.[38]

Through Our Lady we are put in contact with the beauty, truth and goodness of this recreated world, the world as it was meant to be before man's original sin, a world made even more glorious through the life, death, Resurrection and Ascension of Our Lord.

God's forgiveness heals our wounds

Pope Francis wants us to grasp that above all else God wants us to repent of our sins and receive his forgiveness so he can heal our wounds. But we have to let God's forgiveness heal our wounds, he won't force upon us his remedy for inner wounds:

> If we wish to progress in faith, first of all we must receive God's forgiveness; we must meet the Father, who is willing to forgive all things, always, and who precisely in forgiving heals the heart and rekindles love. We must never tire of asking for divine forgiveness, because only when we are forgiven, when we feel we are forgiven, do we learn to forgive.[39]

The Holy Father also wants us to know three life-changing truths about God's forgiveness: God forgives the repentant sinner everything; God never tires of forgiving us; God forgets our sins.

God forgives the repentant sinner everything

As already observed, Pope Francis identifies the loss of the sense of sin as blocking people from seeking the healing of their wounds. He also cautions that being overwhelmed by the sense of sin can also stop us seeking God's forgiveness:

> There is no sin which he won't pardon. He forgives everything. "But Father, I don't go to Confession because

I have committed so many really bad sins, so many that I can't be pardoned." No, this is not true. He forgives everything. If you go (to Confession) repentant, he will forgive everything. When…so many times he doesn't even let you speak! You start to ask for forgiveness and he lets you feel that joy of forgiveness before you have even finished confessing everything.[40]

God never tires of forgiving us

One of the greatest temptations with which the devil can torment us is the mistaken assumption that there is a limit to God's forgiveness. In its most deadly form, this temptation becomes the sin of despair. "By *despair*, man ceases to hope for his personal salvation from God, for help in attaining it or for the forgiveness of his sins" (*CCC* 2091). To counter the danger of despair, Pope Francis says:

The Lord does not disappoint those who take this risk; whenever we take a step towards Jesus, we come to realise that he is already there, waiting for us with open arms. Now is the time to say to Jesus: "Lord, I have let myself be deceived; in a thousand ways I have shunned your love, yet here I am once more, to renew my covenant with you. I need you. Save me once again, Lord, take me once more into your redeeming embrace". How good it feels to come back to him whenever we are lost! Let me say this once more: God never tires of forgiving us; we are the ones who tire of seeking his mercy. Christ, who told us to forgive one another "seventy times seven" (*Mt* 18:22) has given us his example: he has forgiven us seventy times seven.[41]

God forgets our sins

Pope Francis also wants to free us from another illusion that blocks God's deep healing of our wounds. Even though we confess our sins, receive absolution and undertake penance we can be tormented by the memory of our sins. The Holy Father hopes that by knowing that God forgets our sins that this will heal our memories:

There is something beautiful about the way God forgives: God forgets. Scripture also puts it in other words: "Your sins shall be cast into the sea, and though they are red like blood, they shall become white as a lamb" (cf. *Mi* 7:19; *Is* 1:18). Hence, God forgets, and if one of us goes to the Lord and says: "Do you remember, in that year I did something bad?" He answers: "No, no, no. I don't remember". Because once he forgives he no longer remembers, he forgets, while so often, with others, we keep a record: this one did this, another one once did that… But God doesn't do this: he forgives and forgets. However, if he forgets, who am I to remember the sins of others? Thus, the Father forgets, always forgives, forgives all, celebrates when he forgives, and he forgets, because he wants to reconcile, he wants to encounter us.[42]

Some questions to ask ourselves

- Do I admit I am wounded?

- Do I call on Our Lady for help to resist my wounded nature?

- Do I go out to others who are wounded?

- Do I do my best to believe and know the three life-changing truths about God's forgiveness?
  - God forgives the repentant sinner everything;
  - God never tires of forgiving us; and
  - God forgets our sins.

Pope Francis's Advice on Making a Good Confession

Pope Francis has made known his love for the Sacrament of Confession not only through many homilies, addresses and meditations, but also through very visible actions. He is the first pope to make his confession in public - before the world's media at the beginning of a 24-Hour Festival of Forgiveness in 2014. The Holy Father knelt before a priest's open confessional, in St Peter's, confessed his sins for three minutes, and received absolution, with his confessor holding the Pope's hands and kissing his Fisherman's Ring.

During a radio interview Pope Francis confided that he usually goes to Confession every fifteen or twenty days with a Franciscan priest who goes to the Vatican. The Holy Father added: "I never had to call an ambulance to take him back, in shock over my sins!" He finds consolation in the fact that St Peter became pope even though he, too, was a sinner who had committed the serious sin of denying Our Lord. "If they made him pope despite that sin, with all the sins I have, it is a great consolation, because the Lord will look after me as he looked after Peter."[43]

Why is the Sacrament of Confession so important to Pope Francis? Why is Confession such a focus for his words and actions?

In *The Name of God is Mercy,* Pope Francis explores the personal importance of Confession to him. He talks about the confessors who played an important role in his life as a young man, recalling a confession that changed his life: "I think of Father Carlos Duarte Ibarra, the confessor I met in my parish church on 21st September 1953, the day the Church celebrated Saint Matthew the Apostle and Evangelist. I was seventeen years old. On confessing to him, I felt welcomed by the mercy of God."[44]

This experience of the Sacrament of Confession changed Jorge Bergoglio's life and set him on the path to become an apostle of God's mercy and forgiveness. In an interview he gave in 2010, Cardinal Bergoglio gave more details about what happened during this confession:

> In that confession, something very rare happened to me. I don't know what it was, but it changed my life. I would say that I was caught with my guard down... It was a surprise, the astonishment of an encounter. I realised that God was waiting for me. From that moment, for me, God has been the one who precedes [to guide me] ... We want to meet him, but he meets us first.[45]

He further revealed that his breviary contains a manuscript that he composed before his ordination to the priesthood that expresses his personal credo, containing a reference to this encounter with God's mercy in Confession: "I believe in my history - which was pierced by God's look

of love, on the first day of spring, 21st September - he came to meet me and invited me to follow him."[46]

He further explained the impact of this confession on him in an address he gave to two hundred thousand members of Ecclesial Movements in 2013:

One day in particular, though, was very important to me: 21st September 1953. I was almost 17. It was "Students' Day", for us the first day of spring - for you the first day of autumn. Before going to the celebration I passed through the parish I normally attended, I found a priest that I did not know and I felt the need to go to Confession. For me this was an experience of encounter: I found that someone was waiting for me. Yet I do not know what happened, I can't remember, I do not know why that particular priest was there whom I did not know, or why I felt this desire to confess, but the truth is that someone was waiting for me. He had been waiting for me for some time. After making my confession I felt something had changed. I was not the same. I had heard something like a voice, or a call. I was convinced that I should become a priest.[47]

The young Jorge Bergoglio's experience of Confession taught him both the qualities needed in a good confessor and the responses necessary from a good penitent.

The importance of finding a good confessor

Following his confession to Father Carlos Duarte Ibarra, the priest became such an important figure in Jorge Bergoglio's life that when he died only a year later young Jorge was grief stricken. Sixty years later Pope Francis asked himself, why did Father Duarte Ibarra's death have such an impact: "I cried a lot that night, really a lot, and hid in my room. Why? Because I had lost a person who helped me feel the mercy of God".

In his Message for World Youth Day 2016, Pope Francis explains what it was about Fr Carlos Duarte Ibarra that made him such an influential confessor: "I met a priest there who inspired great confidence, and I felt the desire to open my heart in Confession. That meeting changed my life!"[48]

While it is true that it is Our Lord Jesus Christ, not the priest, who absolves us from our sins, the role of the priest as confessor is essential to one's experience of this Sacrament of healing. Pope Francis's life story illustrates a truth known to confessors and spiritual directors for centuries - the importance of finding a good confessor who acts as a sensitive and challenging guide, while at the same time leaving room for the Holy Spirit to work with the penitent. St Francis de Sales viewed the influence of a confessor as so important to the life of a Christian that he said on his deathbed: "Choose a good confessor who shall faithfully teach thee in the way of salvation."

St Francis de Sales also described the relationship between penitent and a good confessor in terms of the love between a child and parent. Pope Francis likewise describes a good confessor as a loving father: "let him find a father who embraces him and says, 'God loves you,' and makes the penitent feel that God really does." In his *Advice to Confessors* St Francis de Sales writes:

> Remember that at the beginning of their confessions the poor penitents call you Father, and that you must indeed have a fatherly heart towards them, receiving them with a great charity, bearing patiently their uncouthness, ignorance, weakness, slowness and other imperfections. Never leave off aiding them and assisting them as long as there is hope of their amendment.

It needs stressing that such parental love towards the penitent does not mean either laxity or severity. St Francis de Sales advised penitents to change confessors who evoked "too much shame or fear". Pope Francis also insists that it's important for confessors to get the balance right:

> And it is necessary to guard against two opposite extremes: rigour and laxity. Neither one is good because in reality they do not take charge of the person of the penitent. Instead mercy listens truly with the heart of God, and wishes to support the soul on the path of reconciliation. Confession is not a court of condemnation, but the experience of forgiveness and mercy![49]

Pope Francis also gave to priests and seminarians this advice on what makes a good confessor, in which one can detect his own experience as that seventeen-year-old penitent:

> To live the Sacrament as a means to educate to mercy means to help our brothers to have the experience of peace and understanding, human and Christian. Confession should not be a "torture", but all should leave the confessional with happiness of heart, with a face radiant with hope even if, sometimes - we know it - bathed by the tears of conversion and of the joy that stems from it. The Sacrament, with all the acts of the penitent, does not imply that it should become a heavy interrogation, annoying and invading. On the contrary, it must be a liberating encounter rich in humanity, through which one can educate to mercy, which does not exclude but rather includes the just commitment to repair, as far as possible, the evil committed. Thus the faithful will feel invited to confess frequently, and will learn to do so in the best of ways, with that delicacy of spirit that has done the heart good - also the heart of the confessor! In this way we priests make the personal relation with God grow, so that his Kingdom of love and peace is dilated in hearts.[50]

The importance of being a good penitent

Jorge Bergoglio's confession to Fr Duarte Ibarra not only taught him the importance of finding a good confessor but also the equal importance of being a good penitent. Looking back at his confession the Holy Father realised that it was not only finding in Fr Duarte Ibarra a priest in whom he could place great confidence, but also that he was willing to open his heart.

Pope Francis understands Confession as a deeply personal encounter, and for this reason warns us not to approach this Sacrament as a visit to the dry cleaner. The Holy Father challenges the mechanical reduction of Confession to an automatic process: "You go in the confessional. You confess your sins. You pray the 'I confess'. The priest absolves you."

Pope Francis wants us to understand that receiving the Sacrament of Reconciliation is not something mechanical that removes the stain of sin like a dry cleaners. This is a superficial approach to Confession that makes the mistake of assuming that going through the motions of Confession, without much thought and self-reflection, is enough to receive the Sacrament of Healing. The Holy Father explains why he calls this 'dry cleaning' understanding of Confession a type of hypocrisy:

> It was an example, an image to explain the hypocrisy of those who believe that sin is a stain, only a stain, something that you can have dry-cleaned so that everything goes back to normal. The way you take a jacket or dress to have a stain removed: you put it in the wash and that's it. But sin is more than a stain. Sin is a wound; it needs to

be treated, healed. This is why I used that expression: I was trying to explain that going to Confession is not like taking your clothes to the dry cleaner.[51]

In order to be good penitents Pope Francis encourages us to adopt four attitudes: honesty about ourselves, acceptance of shame, true repentance and safeguarding your heart.

Honesty about ourselves

If we are to move beyond approaching Confession as a trip to the dry cleaners, Pope Francis encourages us to be honest about ourselves as sinners. Living in the truth is vital to being authentic Christians not only because it is necessary for our wellbeing, but even more because truth is an essential characteristic of God: "To follow Jesus is to live in 'the Spirit of truth', whom the Father sends in his name and who leads 'into all the truth'" (*CCC* 2466). There is no place for insincerity, duplicity, dissimulation or hypocrisy in our lives (*CCC* 2468).

One of Pope Francis's favourite examples of the honest sinner, contrasted with the sinner trapped in hypocrisy, is the woman who washed Our Lord's feet with her tears (*Lk* 7:38). Being honest about her sins led to the loving forgiveness of Jesus:

He only says the word salvation - "Your faith has saved you" - to the woman, who is a sinner. And he says it because she was able to weep for her sins, to confess her sins, to say "I am a sinner", and admit it to herself. He doesn't say the same to those people, who were not bad people: they simply did not believe themselves to be sinners. Other people were sinners: the tax collectors, prostitutes... These were the sinners. Jesus says this word - "You are saved, you are safe" - only to those who open their hearts and acknowledge that they are sinners. Salvation only enters our hearts when we open them to the truth of our sins.[52]

Acceptance of shame

Since St Peter's tears of shame at his betrayal of Our Lord, it has been recognised in Christian spirituality that tears of contrition and penitential tears are a gift from God. There is a tradition of theological and spiritual reflection on the role and significance of compunction, shame and contrition in the penitential experience of God's merciful grace. Unfortunately this rich tradition of spiritual psychology has fallen into disuse in the face of the mistaken Freudian rejection of shame as harmful. Thankfully Pope Francis does not view shame as a taboo, and often refers to the importance of accepting shame in order to benefit from Confession as a sacrament of healing:

I can read my life in light of chapter 16 of the book of the prophet Ezekiel. I read those pages and I say: everything here seems written just for me. The prophet

speaks of shame, and shame is a grace: when one feels
the mercy of God, he feels a great shame for himself
and for his sin… Shame is one of the graces that Saint
Ignatius asks for during his confession of his sins before
Christ crucified. That text from Ezekiel teaches us to be
ashamed, it shows us how to feel shame: with all our
history of wretchedness and sin, God remains faithful
and raises us up. I feel this.[53]

True repentance

One of the most important images of the Christian life
is that of the 'journey'. St Ignatius of Loyola saw the
Christian journey as our participation in Salvation History.
St Teresa of Avila saw it as our journey into the inner
sanctum of the interior castle of the soul. St John of the
Cross saw it as a journey of ascent of Mount Carmel or a
night journey. And St Francis de Sales envisaged each one
of us being presented with a choice - a journey away from
God due to a prodigal heart, or a journey into the interior
of our heart, where God dwells.

All these Saints and masters of the spiritual life agree
that the 'journey' cannot begin unless you experience true
repentance. What is true repentance?

Interior repentance [true repentance] is a radical
reorientation of our whole life, a return, a conversion
to God with all our heart, an end of sin, a turning away

from evil, with repugnance toward the evil actions we have committed. At the same time it entails the desire and resolution to change one's life, with hope in God's mercy and trust in the help of his grace. This conversion of heart is accompanied by a salutary pain and sadness which the Fathers called *animi cruciatus* (affliction of spirit) and *compunctio cordis* (repentance of heart) (*CCC* 1431).

It is a grace from God, which we must be willing to receive and allow to turn our lives upside down. St Ignatius, the founder of the Jesuits, described true repentance as a change of heart: "Interior penance consists in grief for one's sins with the firm determination not to commit again either these or others" (Spiritual Exercises, First Week, Tenth Addition). He held that external penances, such as fasting and mortifications, were only of value if they supported a profound change of heart. As a Jesuit, Pope Francis also stresses the importance of true repentance understood as a change of heart:

It is not the external things that make us holy or unholy, but the heart which expresses our intentions, our choices and the will to do all for the love of God. External behaviour is the result of what we decide in the heart, and not the contrary: with a change in external behaviour, but not a change of heart, we are not true Christians. The boundary between good and evil does not pass outside of us, but rather within us. We could ask ourselves: where is my heart? Jesus said: "Where your treasure is, there will your heart be also." What is my treasure? Is it Jesus, is it his teaching? If so, then the heart is good. Or is my treasure something else? Thus it is a heart which needs purification and conversion. Without a purified heart, one cannot have truly clean hands and lips which speak sincere words of love - it is all duplicitous, a double life - lips which speak words of mercy, of forgiveness: only a sincere and purified heart can do this.[54]

Safeguarding your heart

During his Angelus Address on the first Sunday of Lent 2015, Pope Francis arranged for fifty free copies of a twenty-eight-page booklet called "Safeguard Your Heart" to be handed out to pilgrims in St Peter's Square. As the booklets were being handed out by homeless people, recruited by the Holy See, Pope Francis explained the purpose of the book:

Lent is a journey of conversion that puts the heart at its centre. Our heart must convert to the Lord. Therefore, in this First Sunday, I thought to give those of you who are here in the Square a small booklet entitled "Custodisci il Cuore" ("Guard the Heart"). It's this one. [He holds up the booklet.] This book contains some of Jesus's teaching and the essential contents of our faith, for example the seven Sacraments, the gifts of the Holy Spirit, the ten Commandments, the virtues, the works of mercy…

The volunteers, among whom there are many homeless people who have come on pilgrimage, will now distribute them. And as always, today too, here in the Square, are those who are in need, the same who bring us a great wealth: the wealth of our doctrine, to guard your heart. Each one of you take a booklet and carry it with you, as a help for spiritual conversion and growth that always starts from the heart: the place where the match of daily choices between good and evil is played out, between worldliness and the Gospel, between indifference and sharing. Humanity is in need of justice, of peace, of love and will have it only by returning with their whole heart to God, who is the source of it all. Take the book and read it.[55]

The "heart" is much more than the emotional or feeling dimension of our lives, it is our interior or inner life. Our heart is the core of our being, the place where we enter into dialogue with our self, where we decide whether or not to serve God, where we decide to do good, or do evil. God has made your heart for him. According to St Francis de Sales your heart is the "Temple of God" where God dwells, and which only you, like the High Priest, can enter in order to communicate with God. "God, who probes the heart, awaits him there; there he discerns his proper destiny beneath the eyes of God" (*Gaudium et Spes*, 14).

Be vigilant over your heart

Pope Francis's booklet, "Safeguard Your Heart", contains quotations from the homily he delivered on 10th October 2014 in which the Holy Father reflected on Luke 11:15-26:

> When the unclean spirit has gone out of a man, he passes through waterless places seeking rest; and finding none he says, "I will return to my house from which I came." And when he comes he finds it swept and put in order. Then he goes and brings seven other spirits more evil than himself, and they enter and dwell there; and the last state of that man becomes worse than the first (*Lk* 11:24-26).

Pope Francis takes the existence of the devil very seriously, and wants us to be vigilant against the constant barrage of temptations targeting our hearts. He wants us to know about the tricks that the devil uses so we learn to be on our guard and how to avoid falling for them. The Holy Father asks us to consider "How often do bad thoughts, bad intentions, jealousy, envy enter? Who opened the door? How did those things get in?" He asks us to put a lock on our hearts to stop the entry of the devil's temptations:

> We use many types of security in our houses to defend against thieves. Do we do the same with our heart? Or do we leave the door open? How many times do wicked thoughts enter, wicked intentions, jealousy,

envy. So many things that enter. But who opened that door? Where did they come in? And if we are not aware of whom we let into our heart, it becomes a town square, where everyone comes and goes. You begin to lack intimacy. And there, the Lord cannot speak or even be heard.[56]

The Jesuits have a strong tradition of the daily examination of conscience as a spiritual discipline, which goes back to St Ignatius Loyola. It's not surprising, then, that Pope Francis frequently recommends the practice of a daily examination of conscience for a healthy Christian life. The Holy Father calls it having a "gathered heart" as opposed to a "scattered heart". To have a "gathered heart" means to have "a heart in which we manage to be aware of what's happening... Who among us, in the evening, before the day is over, is alone and in the silence asks himself what has happened in my heart today? What has occurred? What things have passed through my heart?"[57]

Pope Francis's examination of conscience

In his booklet "Safeguard Your Heart" Pope Francis presents an examination of conscience consisting of over thirty questions to help us gather our hearts and lock them against the devil. Here are the Holy Father's questions, to help "one quietly review what bad things one has done and what good things one has failed to do for God, one's neighbour and oneself":

In relation to God

Do I only turn to God when I'm in need?

Do I attend Mass on Sundays and holy days of obligation?

Do I begin and end the day with prayer?

Do I blasphemously misuse the name of God, the Blessed Virgin Mary, the Saints?

Am I ashamed to show that I am a Catholic?

What do I do to grow spiritually, how do I do it, when do I do it?

Do I rebel against God's plan?

Do I pretend that God does my will?

In relation to neighbour

Do I forgive, do I show understanding, do I help my neighbour?

Do I judge without mercy both in thought and in words?

Have I slandered, stolen from or despised the lowly and the defenceless?

Am I envious, hot-tempered, biased?

Am I ashamed of the bodily appearance of my brothers; do I care for the poor and the sick?

Am I honest and fair with everyone or do I fuel the "throwaway culture"?

Have I incited others to do evil?

In my marital and family relations, do I uphold morality as taught in the Gospels?

How do I fulfil my responsibility for the education of my children?

Do I honour and respect my parents?

Have I refused newly conceived life? Have I snuffed out the gift of life? Have I helped do so?

Do I respect the environment?

In relation to ourselves

Am I part worldly and part believer?

Do I overdo it with eating, drinking, smoking and amusements?

Am I overly concerned about my physical well-being, my possessions?

How do I use my time? Am I lazy?

Do I want to be served?

Do I love the culture of purity of heart, of thoughts and of actions?

Do I dream of revenge, hold grudges?

Am I a compassionate and gentle peacemaker?

Through this examination of conscience the Holy Father wants us to learn the vigilance necessary to ensure that the "Spirit doesn't end up in a corner, as if we have locked him in a closet. And there, the Spirit is sad." Instead, if we watch every day our thoughts, feelings and actions we can make sure that the Holy Spirit remains the treasure of our hearts.

Some questions to ask ourselves

- Have I prayed for a good confessor?

- Have I been a good penitent, willing to open my heart to God and to adopt the four attributes of:
  - honesty;
  - shame;
  - repentance; and
  - safeguarding my heart for God?

- Do I put a lock on my heart to stop the entry of the devil's temptations (bad thoughts, bad intentions, jealousy)?

- Do I complete a daily examination of conscience asking: "What has happened in my heart today? What has occurred? What things have passed through my heart?"

Endnotes

[1] Pope Francis, *The Name of God is Mercy*, p. 14.

[2] Radio Message of His Holiness Pius XII to Participants in the National Catechetical Congress of the United States in Boston, 26th October 1946 *https://w2.vatican.va/content/pius-xii/en/speeches/1946/documents/hf_p-xii_spe_19461026_congresso-catechistico-naz.html*

[3] *The Name of God is Mercy*, p. 14.

[4] Morning Meditation in the Chapel of the Domus Sanctae Marthae, 9th October 2015 *https://w2.vatican.va/content/francesco/en/cotidie/2015/documents/papa-francesco-cotidie_20151009_the-well-mannered-evil-one.html*

[5] *The Name of God is Mercy*, pp. 41-42.

[6] Ibid., p. 53.

[7] Ibid., p. 14.

[8] Homily during pastoral visit to the Roman Parish of St Cyril of Alexandria, 1st December 2013 *http://www.catholicnewsagency.com/news/christian-life-is-a-path-of-encountering-jesus-preaches-pope/*

[9] *The Name of God is Mercy*, p. 81.

[10] Fr Antonio Spadro SJ, "A Big Heart Open to God: The exclusive interview with Pope Francis", 30th September 2013 *http://americamagazine.org/pope-interview*

[11] *The Name of God is Mercy*, p. 30.

[12] Ibid., p. 78.

[13] Ibid., p. 40.

[14] Ibid., p. 30.

[15] Angelus, 17th March 2013 *http://w2.vatican.va/content/francesco/en/angelus/2013/documents/papa-francesco_angelus_20130317.html*

[16] General Audience, 9th December 2015 *https://w2.vatican.va/content/francesco/en/audiences/2015/documents/papa-francesco_20151209_udienza-generale.html*

[17] Ibid.

[18] Morning Meditation in the Chapel of the Domus Sanctae Marthae, 10th September 2015 *http://en.radiovaticana.va/news/2015/09/10/pope_francis_a_person_who_can't_forgive_is_not_a_christian/1170862*

[19] Morning Meditation in the Chapel of the Domus Sanctae Marthae, 10th March 2015 *http://en.radiovaticana.va/news/2015/03/10/pope_francis,_to_receive_pardon,_we_must_give_pardon/1128354*

[20] Ibid.

[21] *The Name of God is Mercy*, pp. 93-94.

[22] Morning Meditation in the Chapel of the Domus Sanctae Marthae, 10th March 2015 *http://w2.vatican.va/content/francesco/en/cotidie/2015/documents/papa-francesco-cotidie_20150310_an-open-door.html*

[23] Morning Meditation in the Chapel of the Domus Sanctae Marthae, 10th March 2015 *http://en.radiovaticana.va/news/2015/03/10/pope_francis,_to_receive_pardon,_we_must_give_pardon/1128354*

[24] General Audience, 4th November 2015 *https://w2.vatican.va/content/francesco/en/audiences/2015/documents/papa-francesco_20151104_udienza-generale.html*

[25] Angelus, 26th December 2015 *https://w2.vatican.va/content/francesco/en/angelus/2015/documents/papa-francesco_angelus_20151226.pdf*

[26] Address at Conclusion of the Synod of Bishops, 24th October 2015 *http://w2.vatican.va/content/francesco/en/speeches/2015/october/documents/papa-francesco_20151024_sinodo-conclusione-lavori.html*

[27] General Audience, 13th January 2016 *http://aleteia.org/2016/01/13/full-text-pope-francis-first-wednesday-audience-for-2016-the-name-of-god-is-mercy/*

[28] Ibid.

[29] *The Name of God is Mercy,* p. 4.

[30] Homily on Solemnity of Mary, Most Holy Mother of God, 1st January 2016 *https://w2.vatican.va/content/francesco/en/homilies/2016/documents/papa-francesco_20160101_omelia-giornata-mondiale-pace.html*

[31] Mass for the Faithful of the Armenian Rite, 12th April 2015 *https://w2.vatican.va/content/francesco/en/homilies/2015/documents/papa-francesco_20150412_omelia-fedeli-rito-armeno.html*

[32] Exposition of the Shroud, Video Message, 30th March 2013 *http://w2.vatican.va/content/francesco/en/messages/pont-messages/2013/documents/papa-francesco_20130330_videomessaggio-sindone.html*

[33] Regina Cæli, 19th April 2015 *https://w2.vatican.va/content/francesco/en/angelus/2015/documents/papa-francesco_regina-coeli_20150419.pdf*

[34] *The Name of God is Mercy*, pp. 13-14.

[35] Fr Antonio Spadro SJ, "A Big Heart Open to God: The exclusive interview with Pope Francis", 30th September 2013 *http://americamagazine.org/pope-interview*

[36] Address to Participants in the General Assembly of the Focolare Movement, 26th September 2014 *https://w2.vatican.va/content/francesco /en/speeches/2014/september/documents/papa-francesco_20140926_ movimento-focolari.pdf*

[37] *The Name of God is Mercy*, p. 40.

[38] Angelus, Solemnity of the Immaculate Conception of the Blessed Virgin Mary, 8th December 2015 *https://w2.vatican.va/content/francesco/en/ angelus/2015/documents/papa-francesco_angelus_20151208.html*

[39] Angelus, 26th December 2015 *https://w2.vatican.va/content/francesco/ en/angelus/2015/documents/papa-francesco_angelus_20151226.pdf*

[40] Morning Meditation in the Chapel of the Domus Sanctae Marthae, 23rd January 2015 *http://en.radiovaticana.va/news/2015/01/23/pope_francis_ god_always_forgives_everything/1119557*

[41] Apostolic Exhortation, Evangelii Gaudium, I, 3

[42] Morning Meditation in the Chapel of the Domus Sanctae Marthae, 23rd January 2015 *https://w2.vatican.va/content/francesco/en/cotidie/2015/ documents/papa-francesco-cotidie_20150123_when-god-forgets.html*

[43] Edward Pentin, "Pope Francis: It's Time for Europe 'to Recover Its Faith', 14th September 2015 *https://www.ncregister.com/daily-news/ pope-francis-its-time-for-europe-to-recover-its-faith/blank.htm*

[44] *The Name of God is Mercy*, p. 9.

[45] Fr Roger Landry, "The 60th Anniversary of Pope Francis's Calling", 21st September 2015 *http://www.ncregister.com/site/article/the-60th- anniversary-of-pope-francis-calling*

[46] Ibid.

[47] Vigil of Pentecost with the Ecclesial Movements, 18th May 2013 *https:// w2.vatican.va/content/francesco/en/speeches/2013/may/documents/ papa-francesco_20130518_veglia-pentecoste.html*

[48] Message for the Thirty-First World Youth Day 2016 *http://w2. vatican.va/content/francesco/en/messages/youth/documents/papa- francesco_20150815_messaggio-giovani_2016.html*

[49] Address to Apostolic Penitentiary, 28th March 2014 *https://zenit.org/ articles/pope-francis-address-to-apostolic-penitentiary/*

[50] Address to Participants in a Course on the Internal Forum Organised by the Apostolic Penitentiary, 12th March 2015 *https://zenit.org/articles/ pope-francis-address-to-participants-of-the-course-on-the-internal-forum/*

[51] *The Name of God is Mercy*, p. 24.

[52] Morning Meditation in the Chapel of the Domus Sanctae Marthae, 18th September 2014 *http://en.radiovaticana.va/news/2014/09/18/pope_at_ santa_marta_the_courage_to_admit_we_are_sinners/1106766*
[53] *The Name of God is Mercy*, pp. 8-9.
[54] Angelus, 30th August 2015 *https://w2.vatican.va/content/francesco/en/ angelus/2015/documents/papa-francesco_angelus_20150830.pdf*
[55] Angelus, 22nd February 2015 *https://w2.vatican.va/content/francesco/ en/angelus/2015/documents/papa-francesco_angelus_20150222.html*
[56] Morning Meditation in the Chapel of the Domus Sanctae Marthae, 10th October 2014 *https://w2.vatican.va/content/francesco/en/cotidie/2014/ documents/papa-francesco-cotidie_20141010_the-heart-on-guard.pdf*
[57] Ibid.

Image Credits

Page 7: *The Crucifixion* (oil on canvas), Rubens, Peter Paul (1577-1640) / Ciurlionis State Art Museum, Kaunas, Lithuania / © Leemage / Bridgeman Images

Page 17: Pope Francis hears a confession during a penitential celebration in St. Peter's Basilica © Alessandro Bianchi / POOL/epa/Corbis

Page 36: *Shroud of Turin* © P Deliss/Godong/Corbis

Page 51: Pope Francis receives confession during a penitential celebration in St. Peter's Basilica © Alessandro Bianchi / POOL/epa/Corbis